Flavours of

LINCO

RECIPES

C000053166

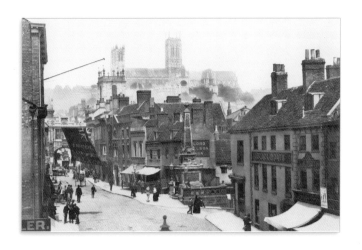

Compiled by Julia Skinner

THE FRANCIS FRITH COLLECTION

www.francisfrith.com

First published in the United Kingdom in 2012 by The Francis Frith Collection®

This edition published exclusively for Bradwell Books in 2013
For trade enquiries see: www.bradwellbooks.com or tel: 0800 834 920
ISBN 978-1-84589-677-5

British Library Cataloguing in Publication Data

Flavours of ... Lincolnshire - Recipes
Compiled by Julia Skinner

The Francis Frith Collection
6 Oakley Business Park,
Wylye Road, Dinton,
Wiltshire SP3 5EU
Tel: +44 (0) 1722 716 376
Email: info@francisfrith.co.uk
www.francisfrith.com

Printed and bound in Malaysia
Contains material sourced from responsibly managed forests

Front Cover: **SKEGNESS, SOUTH PARADE 1899** 44346p
Frontispiece: **LINCOLN, THE CATHEDRAL AND STONEBOW 1890** 25654
Contents: **SCUNTHORPE, GIRLS IN THE HIGH STREET c1960** S78056a

The colour-tinting is for illustrative purposes only, and is not intended to be historically accurate

CONTENTS

BOSTON, DOUGHTY QUAY 1890 26066

The south-east of Lincolnshire is an area of extremely fertile farmland which forms part of the Fens; this is a region of former marshland based mainly around The Wash, which includes part of Lincolnshire, Cambridgeshire and Norfolk. This is a landscape of flat land dominated by vast skies with towering clouds, with drains, dykes and canalised rivers and settlements along banks or on knolls that rise a mere few feet above the surrounding drained marshes, or Fens. The major town of the Lincolnshire Fenland is Boston, which was once one of the most important ports in the country; other towns in this region include Spalding and market towns such as Holbeach, Long Sutton and Bourne.

BOURNE, NORTH STREET 1952 B511003

RECIPE

PEA SOUP

The rich, silty soil of the Lincolnshire Fens is particularly suited to vegetable growing, with pea cultivation being especially important. Pea pods have an intense flavour, and this recipe ensures that this is not wasted.

450g/1 lb fresh peas in their pods
1 onion
50g/2oz butter
900ml/1½ pints good ham or vegetable stock
1 teaspoonful of sugar
2 sprigs of fresh mint
1 teaspoonful of cornflour
300ml/ ½ pint milk
Salt and pepper

Shell the peas, wash the empty pods and remove the stringy edge and any other hard, fibrous bits. Peel and finely chop the onion. Melt the butter in a large heavy saucepan, add the peas, pods and chopped onion and fry gently for a few minutes until softened. Add the stock, sugar and sprigs of mint. Bring to the boil, then reduce the heat, cover and simmer until the peas and pods are tender. Blend the cornflour with a little milk and stir it into the soup, together with the remaining milk. Increase the heat and bring the soup back to the boil, stirring all the time. Remove from heat and allow to cool for a few minutes, then liquidize the soup in a blender or pass it through a sieve. Season the soup with salt and pepper to taste, and reheat before serving.

HOLBEACH, HIGH STREET c1955 H318015

A root vegetable grown in Lincolnshire is celeriac, which tastes delicious but is known for its unattractive appearance – so much so that the celeriac grown and sold as a niche crop by Jack Buck (Farms) Ltd at Moulton Seas End, west of Holbeach, is marketed as 'The Ugly One'. Celeriac is the edible root of a variety of celery. Beneath its brown, fibrous skin is creamy-white flesh that is full of flavour, and celeriac deserves to be more widely eaten than it is at present. British celeriac is in season from October to March. Celeriac is delicious eaten as a vegetable dish, either mashed, puréed, or sliced and baked with potatoes as a 'Dauphinoise' in a creamy sauce, but it also makes the delicious soup on the opposite page, which is quick and easy to prepare.

RECITE

CELERIAC SOUP

1 whole medium-sized celeriac, about 570g/1 lb 4oz – to give
  about 450g/1 lb in prepared weight when trimmed and peeled
2 onions
2 cloves of garlic
1 tablespoonful cooking oil
600ml/1 pint chicken or vegetable stock
A handful of fresh thyme leaves, picked off their stalks (or 1
  teaspoonful of dried thyme if necessary, but fresh thyme is best)
Salt and freshly ground black pepper to taste
150ml/5fl oz single cream, natural yogurt or crème fraîche to finish
Very finely chopped fresh parsley, to garnish

Peel the celeriac and chop it into small chunks. Peel and finely chop
the onions, and peel and finely chop or crush the garlic cloves. Heat
the oil in a large pan and gently fry the onion and garlic for a few
minutes, then add the chopped celeriac and cook over a medium
heat for about 15 minutes, stirring occasionally, until the celeriac is
beginning to soften. Add the stock and thyme leaves, and season
with salt and freshly ground black pepper. Bring to the boil, then
reduce and leave to simmer gently for one hour. Remove from
the heat and allow to cool a little, then liquidize or pass through
a blender in batches until smooth, then push the soup through a
sieve for a really velvety finish and to remove any thyme stalks that
might have found their way into the mixture. Put the soup back in
the cleaned out pan, and adjust the seasoning to taste with salt and
freshly ground black pepper. Reheat and serve in individual bowls
with a swirl of cream, natural yogurt or crème fraîche on top and a
garnish of very finely chopped fresh parsley.
If the soup comes out too thick for your taste, add a little milk to thin
it to the required consistency and warm through.

GRIMSBY, THE DOCKS 1893 33272

By the 1920s Grimsby in Lincolnshire had grown into the largest and most prosperous fishing port in the world. A huge tonnage of cod, haddock and herring from the North Sea and the Icelandic fishing grounds was processed in the town to supply the length and breadth of the nation. During the inter-war years there was exceptional growth of the steam trawler fleet based in Grimsby, and these ships, with their port registration letter 'GY' for Grimsby, are seen in many photographs of the docks at this time. It is an astonishing fact that Grimsby alone, from this time and until the mid 1970s, provided one fifth of all the fish consumed in the UK. The eventual decline in the industry came as a result of the fishing limitations that Iceland placed on their fishing ground, which resulted in the aptly named 'cod wars' of the 1970s. The outcome was a huge decline in fish landings and the eventual loss of Grimsby's own deep sea trawling fleet.

Fortunately though, Grimsby people adapt. Smaller shallow-water seine fishermen took over, and with a substantial fresh fish processing and cold storage facility in town, fish is still brought to Grimsby for sale and processing. Trade in the town's state-of-the-art fish market is busy, and Grimsby is now both the UK centre for buying, selling and freezing fish, and one of Europe's premier fishing and fish processing centres, with the largest frozen storage capacity in Europe.

Appropriately for a place with such a strong fishing tradition, the multi-award-winning National Fishing Heritage Centre opened at the Alexandra Dock at Grimsby in 1991. The trawler 'Ross Tiger', which is moored outside the centre, is an excellent reminder of the proud heritage that built the town.

GRIMSBY, THE FISH PONTOON 1906 55749

RECIPE

COD AND LIME FISHCAKES

This recipe is a reminder of Grimsby's deep-water cod-fishing tradition. However, nowadays cod is getting scarce and is expensive, so you might prefer to use an alternative and more sustainable fish variety instead, such as haddock, hake, coley or salmon – or a combination of several types of fish.

> 750g/1½ lbs thick cod fillet (or alternative fish – see above)
> 450g/1 lb large new potatoes, scrubbed and parboiled until they are tender
> Half an onion, grated
> Grated zest of 1 lemon and 1 lime
> Juice of 1 lime
> Salt and freshly ground black pepper
> 2 tablespoonfuls sunflower oil

Place the fish fillet in a pan, and cover with water. Heat until the water simmers for 2 minutes, then turn off the heat, cover the pan and leave to cool. Alternatively the fish can be cooked in a microwave, covered with film, on a high setting for about 3 minutes, and then left to cool. When cooked and cooled, flake the fish into large pieces.

Grate the potatoes into a bowl, and add the flaked fish and grated onion, the lemon and lime zest and lime juice. Season with salt and freshly ground black pepper to taste. Shape the mixture with your hands on a floured surface into 8 thick fishcakes, place them on a plate and leave to rest in the fridge for 10 minutes.

Heat the oil in a frying pan and fry the fish cakes on one side until they are crusty and browned, then turn each fishcake and cook the other side.

GRIMSBY, 'LINDY-SUE' AND THE FISH DOCKS c1965   G60063x

RECIPE

FISHERMAN'S PIE

The recipe for this fish pie uses smoked haddock which together with smoked cod has become a local speciality of Grimsby. At one time there were nearly 80 fish smoke-houses around Grimsby. Now only a handful of traditional smoke-houses remain, but they still process fish with great skill, producing a smoked fish product in the time-honoured way with a distinctive texture and fabulous flavour that is dependant on the type of wood used in the cold smoking process, wood quality, smoke time and temperature control. The smokehouses in Grimsby also have the great advantage of using freshly-caught fish that comes to them direct from the local fish markets each day. In 2009, following a long campaign by the Grimsby Traditional Fish Smokers Group to gain recognition for their product, Traditional Grimsby smoked fish was awarded a Protected Geographical Indication (PGI) by the European Commission, meaning that only fish processed according to the traditional smoking methods within a defined geographical area around Grimsby can use that name. For more delicious recipes using Traditional Grimsby smoked fish, see the website of the Grimsby Traditional Fish Smokers Group: www.gtfsgroup.co.uk

<u>For the filling:</u>
350ml/12 fl oz milk
1 bay leaf
Half an onion, finely sliced
450g/1 lb haddock or cod fillet
225g/8oz Traditional Grimsby smoked haddock fillet
3 hard-boiled eggs, shelled and chopped into small pieces
25g/1oz butter or margarine
25g/1oz plain flour
75g/3oz shelled prawns
2 tablespoonfuls chopped fresh parsley
Lemon juice to taste

For the topping:
500g/1¼ lbs potatoes, cooked
40g/1½ oz butter
60ml/4 tablespoonfuls milk
115g/4oz grated hard cheese of choice
Salt and pepper

Place the milk, bay leaf and sliced onion in a saucepan over a medium heat and add the fish. Cover, and poach the fish lightly for 10 minutes. Discard the bay leaf and strain, reserving the milk for the sauce. Flake the fish into a buttered pie dish, discarding the skin and any remaining bones. Add the chopped hard-boiled eggs to the fish.

Melt 25g/1oz butter in a saucepan on a low heat, stir in the flour and cook gently for 1 minute, stirring continually. Remove the pan from the heat and stir in the reserved milk that the fish was poached in, a little at a time and stirring continually so that no lumps are formed. When all the milk has been mixed in, return the pan to the heat and bring the mixture to the boil, stirring continually as the sauce thickens, then simmer the sauce for about 4 minutes, still stirring all the time. Remove from the heat and stir in the prawns. Add the parsley, lemon juice and seasoning to taste. Pour the sauce over the fish and eggs in the pie dish, and gently mix it all together.

Pre-heat the oven to 180°C/350°F/Gas Mark 4.

Now make the topping: gently heat 40g/1½ oz butter in 60ml/4 tablespoonfuls of milk in a small saucepan until the butter melts, then add the milk and melted butter to the cooked potatoes, mash and then beat until smooth. Spoon the topping over the fish pie mixture to cover, and score the surface with a fork. Sprinkle the grated cheese over the pie before baking. Bake the pie in the pre-heated oven for 25-30 minutes, until the top is golden.

RECIPE

HERRINGS WITH MUSTARD SAUCE

Herrings are still caught in autumn off the Lincolnshire coast, although not in the huge numbers that they were caught in the past. In this recipe, they are served with a savoury stuffing for a tasty lunch or supper. Mustard sauce is a traditional accompaniment to herrings in many parts of England, with the sharpness of the mustard cutting through the oiliness of the fish. The use of mustard with herrings is said to have been a culinary tradition introduced by the Vikings, such as the Danish raiders who settled in the Lincolnshire area over a thousand years ago. After the Peace of Wedmore of AD886 between the Anglo-Saxon King Alfred the Great and the Danish leader Guthram, England was divided up into two halves; the southern half remained under Anglo-Saxon rule, and the other became the 'Danelaw', which was under Danish control. Two of the important 'Five Boroughs' of the Danelaw were in Lincolnshire, the settlements of Stamford and Lincoln (the other three were Derby, Nottingham and Leicester). That Viking-Danish heritage is recalled in hundreds of place names around Lincolnshire, particularly those ending in '-by', '-toft', '-thorpe' and '-ness', meaning respectively 'town' or 'village', 'homestead', 'hamlet', and 'headland'. The name of Skegness probably means 'Skeggi's headland', named after a Viking settler called Skeggi. Originally a small fishing village, the railway arrived in Skegness in 1873, and thereafter the town was very much developed with day trips and excursions in mind. Skegness was famously promoted by the well-known jolly fisherman character designed in 1908 by John Hassell for use on a poster for the Great Northern Railway to publicise the resort; the poster featured a portly fisherman dressed in seaboots happily skipping across the sands at Skegness, together with the slogan 'Skegness is so Bracing'. Bracing is a good word to describe the north and east winds that frequently blow into the coast there, but the sandy beaches are superb compensation. A bronze statue by Ron Walker of the jolly fisherman character, unveiled in 1989 and known locally as 'Jolly', stands on the seafront of the resort.

4 large herrings
3 heaped tablespoonfuls fresh white breadcrumbs
1 heaped teaspoonful finely chopped parsley
A squeeze of lemon juice
Grated rind of half a lemon
Salt and black pepper
Oil for brushing the fish
25g/1oz butter

<u>Mustard Sauce</u>
40g/1½ oz butter
25g/1oz plain flour
450ml/ ¾ pint milk
Salt and freshly ground black pepper
1 level tablespoonful dry mustard powder
1 tablespoonful wine vinegar
1 level teaspoonful caster sugar
Lemon wedges and fresh parsley sprigs for garnish

Remove the heads from the herrings, clean, gut and bone them. Wash the herrings and pat them dry. Put the breadcrumbs, parsley, lemon juice and rind in a basin, and season lightly with salt and pepper. Melt the butter and stir into the breadcrumbs to bind the mixture, which should be moist, but crumbly. Stuff the herrings with the breadcrumb mixture, and secure them with wooden cocktail sticks. Slash the skins crossways two or three times on each side; brush the herrings with oil and wrap each in foil. Put the herrings in a well-buttered deep baking dish; cover with buttered greaseproof paper and bake in a pre-heated oven at 200°C/400°F/Gas Mark 6 for 35-40 minutes.

For the sauce, melt 25g/1oz of the butter in a pan; stir in the flour and cook for 1 minute. Gradually stir in the milk, beating well until the sauce is smooth. Bring to the boil and simmer for 2-3 minutes; season with salt and pepper. Blend the mustard powder with the vinegar and stir into the sauce; add the sugar. Check seasoning and stir in the remaining butter.

SKEGNESS, FROM THE PIER 1910 62843

RECIPE

LINCOLNSHIRE BEEF BRAISED IN BEER
WITH HERB DUMPLINGS

The Lincoln Red is one of England's oldest beef breeds, producing a
succulent meat with an excellent flavour. Use one of the many fine
Lincolnshire-brewed beers to make this an even more authentic local dish.

<u>For the stew:</u>
25g/1oz butter
2 tablespoonfuls oil
115g/4oz streaky bacon, chopped into small pieces
900g/2 lbs Lincoln Red braising steak, cut into chunks
3 tablespoonfuls plain flour
450ml/ ¾ pint beer
450ml/ ¾ pint beef stock
1 bouquet garni
8 shallots or very small onions
175g/6oz button mushrooms
Salt and freshly ground black pepper

<u>For the dumplings:</u>
115g/4oz self-raising flour
50g/2oz shredded suet
Half a teaspoonful salt
Half a teaspoonful mustard powder
1 tablespoonful chopped fresh parsley
1 tablespoonful chopped fresh thyme

Melt half the butter with half the oil in a large heavy frying pan, add the
bacon pieces and brown on both sides. Transfer the cooked bacon to a
casserole dish. Brown the meat chunks in the frying pan in batches, a few
pieces at a time, transferring them to the casserole when browned. Stir
the flour into the remaining fat in the frying pan. Gradually add the beer
and stock, stirring continually to mix it well together. Season to taste,
then bring to the boil, constantly stirring as it thickens. Pour the sauce

over the meat in the casserole dish and add the bouquet garni. Cover the casserole with its lid, and place it in a cold oven. Set the oven temperature to 200°C/400°F/Gas Mark 6. Cook for 30 minutes, then reduce the temperature to 160°C/325°F/Gas Mark 3 and cook for a further 1 hour.

Heat the remaining butter and oil in a frying pan and cook the shallots or onions until they are golden. Take the onions out of the pan, add the mushrooms and cook quickly for 2-3 minutes. Add the onions and mushrooms to the casserole and cook for a further 30 minutes, then make the dumplings. Mix together the dumpling ingredients in a bowl, then add enough cold water to form a soft dough. Flour your hands and roll the mixture into about 12 balls, and place them on top of the stew. Replace the casserole lid and cook the stew for 25-30 minutes more, then serve piping hot.

SCUNTHORPE, HIGH STREET
1904 52160v

STAMFORD, RED LION SQUARE
1922 72300

Stamford is one of England's most attractive and historic towns. An ancient trackway once crossed the River Welland by the stone ford that gave the town its name. This photograph shows Stamford's High Street as it appeared in 1922. The gabled building second from the left in the photograph was the premises of J Grant, Family Butcher, which was still trading in the town at that time. Grant's butcher's shop was dismantled in 1936 and the building was moved to York, where it was reconstructed in the York Castle Museum to form part of the museum's famous Victorian street scene, 'Kirkgate'. Thus it is now possible to visit an old Stamford butcher's shop in the heart of Yorkshire!

STAMFORD, HIGH STREET 1922 72302

LINCOLNSHIRE STUFFED CHINE

Stuffed chine is a speciality of Lincolnshire, a celebratory dish which was enjoyed at important events such as weddings and christenings and was also the traditional fare for May Day. The chine (a cut from the back of the pig) was cured for several weeks in salt and saltpetre, and then was slashed with a knife to form 'pockets' in the meat which were stuffed with whatever was to hand; although parsley was the most usual ingredient, lettuce, nettles, onion, sage, leeks, herbs and onion tops might also be used. The chine would then either be baked in a pastry case or tied up in a cloth and simmered for several hours.

In his book 'Hedingham Harvest', a chronicle of life in a (fictional) north Lincolnshire village in Victorian times, Geoffrey Robinson gave an evocative description of how his grandmother prepared her version of Lincolnshire stuffed chine, describing how she left the chine to stand for about a month for the salt and saltpetre to soak in. It was then hung for several more weeks. When it was dry, deep clefts would be cut in the chine which were stuffed with a mixture of finely chopped parsley, marjoram, thyme, chives and – most importantly – exactly 3 blackcurrant leaves. The rows of clefts filled with greenstuff gave the chine a striped appearance evocative of lines of crops sprouting in the fields in springtime. The chine was then baked in a pastry crust which was broken off and thrown away when the chine was ready for eating. The chine was always eaten cold, accompanied by an 'old-fashioned salad' made of lettuce leaves with chopped spring onions, sugar, salt and pepper, all of which was soaked in vinegar for an hour before eating.

RECIPE

LINCOLNSHIRE HASLET

Lincolnshire Haslet (pronounced 'hacelet' locally) is a traditional meat loaf made with pork and seasoned with sage.

> 175g/6oz pigs' liver
> 175g/6oz lean and fat bits of pork
> 75g/3oz pigs' heart
> 1 small onion
> 50g/2oz fresh breadcrumbs
> 2-3 leaves of fresh sage, chopped
> 1 teaspoonful salt
> Pepper

Mince the liver, pork, heart and onion. Add the breadcrumbs and sage, and season with salt and pepper. Mix all together into a loaf shape, then wrap in foil and place on a small baking tray. Cook in a moderate oven, 180°C/350°F/Gas Mark 4, for about 1½ hours.

SPILSBY, THE FRANKLIN MONUMENT 1956 S391007

TOAD IN THE HOLE WITH LINCOLNSHIRE SAUSAGES

Lincolnshire has its own distinctive variety of pork sausage that has a dominant flavour of herbs, with sage being the traditional flavouring. Lincolnshire Sausages are also notable for having an open, chunky texture, being made with pork that is coarsely ground, rather than minced.

> 450g/1 lb Lincolnshire sausages
> 175g/6oz plain flour
> A pinch of salt
> 2 eggs
> 600ml/1 pint milk and water mixed
> 15g/ ½ oz lard or dripping

Make the batter 1 hour before you start cooking the dish. Put the flour in a bowl with the salt, make a well in the centre and break in the eggs. Beat them into the flour, gradually adding the milk and water to make a smooth, creamy batter. Beat it well, then leave to stand for 1 hour. (This can also be prepared in a liquidizer.)

Pre-heat the oven to 220°C/425°F/Gas Mark 7. Melt the lard or dripping in a frying pan and brown the sausages nicely all over (this gives a better flavour than cooking the sausages in the oven). Pour the fat and sausages into a roasting tin. Place the tin in the oven for a few minutes to heat through, then remove from the oven, pour in the prepared batter and replace the tin in the oven. When the batter is nicely puffed up, reduce the oven temperature to 190°C/375°F/Gas Mark 5, and continue cooking until well-risen and golden brown – the total cooking time from start to finish should be 35-40 minutes.

Geese were bred in great numbers on the Lincolnshire fens in the past, and were so important to the local economy that they were known as 'the fenman's treasurer'. In 1861 Mrs Beeton wrote in her 'Book of Household Management that 'The best geese are found on the borders of Suffolk, and in Norfolk and Berkshire; but the largest flocks are reared in the fens of Lincolnshire and Cambridgeshire – large herds of them are sent every year to London'. In arable regions such as these, geese were fattened on stubble after the wheat harvest and then driven on foot in great droves to the London markets. In Lincolnshire the feathers of the geese were plucked twice a year to fill feather beds and pillows, and in the 19th and 20th centuries Boston was the centre of the fenland feather industry, with several factories there purifying feathers for pillows and other purposes. Now the only business left in this industry in Boston is Fogarty's, established in Boston in 1877, which also uses man-made fillers.

BOSTON, MARKET PLACE AND CHURCH
1890 26068

RECIPE

TRADITIONAL ROAST GOOSE

In the western Christian religious calendar, the feast day of
St Michael the Archangel on 29th September is known as
Michaelmas Day. This was an important day in the past, and as it
coincided with the time when geese first became ready to eat,
after fattening on the corn stubble after harvest time, it became
traditional to eat roast goose at Michaelmas. There was a saying
that if you ate goose on this day you would not want for money
for the following year:

> *'Whoever eats goose on Michaelmas Day*
> *Shall never lack money for his debts to pay.'*

1 goose (keep a note of its weight)
115g/4oz pork
115g/4oz veal
1 large onion
A small knob of butter
2 slices of bread soaked in milk
1 egg yolk
Parsley, thyme, sage, finely chopped
3fl oz/75ml red wine

Make a stuffing by chopping the pork, veal, onion and the goose
liver very finely and brown them in the butter. Squeeze the milk
out of the bread and mix together all the ingredients except
the wine, and using only a little of the wine to moisten. Season
with salt and pepper to taste. Stuff the goose with the mixture
and put it into a very hot oven, about 230°C/450°F/Gas Mark 8,
for 15 minutes. Reduce the heat to 180°C/350°F/Gas Mark 4, and
cook for a further 15 minutes per 450g/1 lb weight of the goose,
basting with the remaining wine and juices in the roasting dish.

RECIPE

CHEESE PUDDING

Cheese Pudding has long been popular in Lincolnshire, East Anglia and the Midlands. It is a rich and tasty dish which is good eaten either hot or cold, perhaps served with brown bread and butter, or with a salad. The secret to a good Cheese Pudding is to use a tasty, well-flavoured cheese of choice. Serves 4.

> 225g/8oz hard cheese such as Cheddar, Cheshire, Double Gloucester or Lancashire, grated
> 4 eggs
> ¼ teaspoonful Cayenne pepper
> ¼ teaspoon freshly grated nutmeg
> A pinch of salt
> Freshly ground black pepper
> 150ml/5fl oz single cream

Pre-heat the oven to 180°C/350°F/Gas Mark 4. Grease an ovenproof dish of about 900ml (1½ pints) capacity. Break the eggs into a large bowl and beat them well. Mix in the grated cheese, Cayenne pepper, nutmeg, black pepper, and a little salt – the cheese already makes the dish salty. Add the cream, and beat the mixture well. Pour into the greased dish and bake in the centre of the oven for 25-30 minutes, until the pudding is well risen and firm to the touch, and the top is starting to brown.

MARKET DEEPING, MARKET PLACE 1900 M116301

RECIPE

BRUSSELS SPROUTS WITH BACON

Lincolnshire is England's premier agricultural county, and as it is on the eastern side of the country, it is one of the driest – hence most of its flat, fertile land is used for arable farming. The usual crops are wheat, barley, potatoes, oil seed rape, linseed, peas and millions of cabbages, but cauliflowers, broccoli, carrots, onions and Brussels sprouts are also important crops. Lincolnshire is one of England's main producers of Brussels sprouts. This way of preparing sprouts makes a tasty starter or supper dish, or an unusual way of serving them as a vegetable accompaniment to meat as a main course.

675g/1½ lbs Brussels sprouts
6 rashers of streaky bacon
75g/3oz cheese of choice
25g/1oz fresh breadcrumbs

Wash and trim the Brussels sprouts, then cook them in boiling water until tender. Drain and put to one side. Chop the bacon into pieces and fry them for 10 minutes until they are cooked, then place the cooked bacon pieces in an ovenproof dish.

Toss the Brussels sprouts in the bacon fat left in the pan to coat them, then add them to the bacon in the dish. Grate the cheese and mix it with the breadcrumbs, and sprinkle the mixture on top of the sprouts and bacon.

Place the dish under a hot grill to brown the topping, and serve hot.

STUFFED ONIONS WITH LINCOLNSHIRE POACHER CHEESE

In this recipe, onions are teamed with the award-winning Lincolnshire Poacher Cheese made by F W Read & Sons Ltd of Ulceby Grange near Alford, on the eastern edge of the Lincolnshire Wolds. Lincolnshire Poacher Cheese (named after a famous Lincolnshire folk song) is an unpasteurised cheese that is handmade from a traditional recipe only between the months of October and May. It is matured for an exceptionally long time – 15 to 18 months – to produce a flavoursome, full bodied cheese which was judged to be of Gold Medal standard at the British Cheese Awards in 2001.

4 large onions
50g/2oz fresh breadcrumbs
50g/2oz bacon, finely chopped
1 teaspoonful of fresh sage leaves, finely chopped
Salt and pepper to taste
25g/1oz butter
25g/1oz grated Lincolnshire Poacher Cheese
A little chopped fresh parsley to garnish

Remove the onion skins, but keep the onions whole. Place the onions in a large pan of boiling water, and boil for 20 minutes until they are softened.

Pre-heat the oven to 200°C/400°F/Gas Mark 6.

Remove the onions from the pan and drain, then leave to cool for a few minutes. Cut the top of each onion, then scoop out the centre and finely chop. Mix together the chopped cooked onions, breadcrumbs, bacon and sage, and season to taste, then mix in the butter well. Use the mixture to fill each onion shell, and sprinkle the tops with the grated cheese. Stand the onions on a baking tray, and bake in the pre-heated oven for about 30 minutes. Serve garnished with the chopped parsley.

RECIPE

LINCOLNSHIRE STOVIES

This is another recipe celebrating Lincolnshire's vegetable growing heritage, this time using potatoes to make a tasty supper dish to eat either by itself or to serve with bacon or sausage as a vegetable accompaniment. Why not use Lincolnshire Poacher cheese to make this? Otherwise use a tasty, well-flavoured hard cheese of choice.

> 800g/1¾ lb potatoes, peeled and cut into thin slices
> 2 onions, peeled and cut into thin slices
> 50g/2oz butter or margarine
> 50g/2oz plain flour
> 425ml/ ¾ pint chicken or vegetable stock
> 425ml/ ¾ pint milk
> Salt and pepper to taste
> 1 teaspoonful very finely chopped fresh sage leaves
> 75g/3oz grated hard cheese of choice (see above)

Grease a large oven-proof dish and pre-heat the oven to 200°C/400°/ Gas Mark 6. Fill the dish with alternating layers of the sliced potatoes and sliced onions, finishing with a layer of potatoes. Melt the butter or margarine in saucepan over a medium heat, stir in the flour and cook gently for 2 minutes. Add the milk a little at a time, stirring or whisking continually so that no lumps are formed. Mix in the chicken or vegetable stock and bring to the boil, stirring constantly, until the sauce thickens. Reduce the heat, season well to taste with salt and pepper and simmer the sauce gently for 2 minutes. Pour the sauce over the vegetables in the dish, then give the dish a good shake to distribute the sauce evenly. Sprinkle the chopped sage over the top, then cover with the grated cheese.

Cover the dish with its lid, or with a tightly-fitted piece of kitchen foil, and bake in the pre-heated oven for one hour, then remove the lid or foil, reduce the oven temperature to 150°C/325°F/Gas Mark 4 and bake for a further one hour, until the top is lightly browned and the vegetables are cooked through.

RECIPE

CAULIFLOWER SOUFFLÉ FLAN

Lincolnshire is one of the main cauliflower-growing regions of the UK. This is a tasty savoury flan made with cauliflower that can either be eaten hot or cold.

<u>For the pastry:</u>
225g/8oz plain flour
115g/4oz butter or margarine
A pinch of salt

<u>For the filling:</u>
1 small cauliflower, trimmed and cut into florets
25g/1oz butter or margarine
2 tablespoonfuls flour
300ml/ ½ pint milk
1 dessertspoonful wholegrain mustard
150ml/ ¼ pint double cream
1 large egg, separated
Salt and freshly ground black pepper, to taste
75g/3oz Cheddar cheese, grated
1 tablespoonful fine fresh breadcrumbs
A little extra butter to finish, dotted over the surface

Put the flour into a mixing bowl with a pinch of salt, and rub in the butter or margarine with your fingertips until the mixture resembles fine breadcrumbs. Add 2-3 tablespoonfuls of cold water, just enough to mix it all together to form a firm dough, then knead the dough lightly until it is smooth and elastic. Wrap the pastry in cling film or put it inside a plastic bag and leave in the fridge to chill for 30 minutes.

Pre-heat the oven to 200°C/400°F/Gas Mark 6 and grease a flan dish or tin 22-24cms (9-10 ins) in diameter.

Roll out the pastry on a lightly floured surface and use it to line the flan dish or tin. Prick the pastry base all over with a fork, to allow air bubbles to escape during cooking. Line the pastry case with a piece of greaseproof paper or kitchen foil and fill it with baking beans (or alternative, such as uncooked rice). Place in the oven and bake blind for 10 minutes, until the pastry is just firm and lightly golden. Remove from the oven, take out the baking beans and paper or foil and return the dish or tin to the oven for a further 5 minutes to dry out the pastry base. Remove from the oven, and reduce the oven temperature to 190°C/375°F/Gas Mark 5.

Bring a saucepan of salted water to the boil and add the cauliflower florets. Cover the pan and simmer rapidly for about 10 minutes, until the florets are tender, then drain them very well.

Now make a white sauce. Melt the butter or margarine in a saucepan, then stir in the flour. Gradually stir in the milk, a little at a time, then bring to the boil, stirring continually, until the mixture boils and is thick and smooth. Reduce the heat and simmer for 2 minutes. Stir in the mustard, and season to taste with salt and freshly ground black pepper. Leave to cool a little, then stir in the cream and egg yolk. Whisk the egg white in a small bowl until it is stiff, then use a large metal spoon to fold it gently into the sauce mixture.

Arrange the cooked cauliflower florets on the pastry base of the flan, and pour over the sauce. Sprinkle the grated cheese and then the breadcrumbs over the top. Dot the surface with small dots of butter, then bake in the oven at the reduced temperature for 25-30 minutes, until the filling is risen and firm.

RECIPE

ROAST PUMPKIN

Lincolnshire is famous for growing spring bulbs and daffodils, especially around Spalding and Holbeach. However, Spalding has also become famous in recent years for the pumpkin festival that is held in the town every October.

Pumpkin is probably best known for making a wonderful soup, but it also makes a delicious vegetable dish with a sweet flavour when simply roasted in the oven like this. Serves 4-6.

> 1 medium pumpkin, about 24cms (6-9 inches) in diameter
> 3 tablespoonfuls olive oil
> A handful of fresh sage leaves (left whole, not chopped)
> Salt and freshly ground black pepper
> Half a teaspoonful freshly grated nutmeg

Pre-heat the oven to 200°C/400°F/Gas Mark 6.

Peel the pumpkin, de-seed it and cut the flesh into chunks or slices about 4cm (1½ inches) thick. Put the pumpkin pieces into a large roasting tin with 2 tablespoonfuls of the olive oil, season with salt and pepper, and toss the pieces in the oil so that all the sides are coated. Roast the pumpkin in the pre-heated oven for 35-40 minutes, or until the pieces are golden and tender when tested with a skewer or the point of a sharp knife, turning them once during the cooking time. Add the sage leaves to the tin for the last 5 minutes of the cooking time. Remove the tin from the oven, drizzle the rest of the olive oil over the pumpkin pieces and grate a little nutmeg over them. Serve straight away.

RECIPE

OVEN-BAKED CARROTS WITH HONEY AND MUSTARD

Lincolnshire is also one of the country's main carrot growing areas. Carrots are very good for you, being rich in beta carotene, which the body converts to vitamin A – a crucial nutrient for maintaining proper eyesight – as well being a good source of dietary fibre, antioxidants, and minerals. This is not a traditional Lincolnshire recipe, but it is an unusual and delicious way of cooking carrots to serve as a vegetable accompaniment, which gives them a wonderful flavour.

> 450g/1 lb carrots
> 2 tablespoonfuls of water
> 2 tablespoonfuls of sunflower oil
> 2 tablespoonfuls of runny honey
> 1 tablespoonful of wholegrain mustard
> Salt and freshly ground black pepper

Pre-heat the oven to 190°C/375°F/Gas Mark 5. Scrub the carrots and trim off the ends, then chop them into chunky sticks.
Put the carrot pieces into a shallow ovenproof dish. In a bowl, mix together the water, oil, honey and mustard, and season to taste with a little salt and freshly ground black pepper. Pour the mixture over the carrots in the oven dish, and stir until the carrots have all been coated with the mixture.

Cover the dish with its lid, or a piece of close-fitting kitchen foil, and bake in the pre-heated oven for 50-60 minutes, until the carrots are tender.

CLEETHORPES, THE FLYING MACHINE 1906 55735

A wild plant called Marsh Samphire, or glasswort, is found growing on the salt marshes around the coast of Lincolnshire, especially around The Wash, and has been eaten as a delicacy by local people for centuries. It is often known as 'poor man's asparagus'. The green fleshy tips of this succulent, bright green plant should be washed and trimmed of any coarse roots, then steamed or cooked in boiling water for 6-8 minutes, until tender but still with some 'bite' to it. Samphire can either be served hot, with melted butter, or cold in a salad, with a vinaigrette dressing. It goes very well with lamb, fish and shellfish.

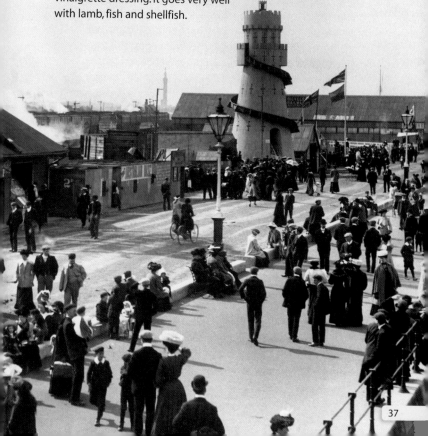

RECIPE

LINCOLNSHIRE POTATO CHEESECAKE

In the past, root vegetables like carrots, parsnips and potatoes were often used as an ingredient in sweet puddings or pies that were eaten as dessert dishes. This is an old Lincolnshire recipe for a sweet dessert dish made with potatoes, which was traditionally served at Harvest Home suppers. Although it is called a cheesecake, it does not actually contain any cheese, but was so-called because the filling resembles the old-fashioned Tudor-style cheesecakes of the past. These older-style 'cheesecakes' were not the creamy desserts on a biscuit base that we know today, but small cakes baked in a pastry case with a filling originally made of curd cheese and dried fruit. Over the centuries enterprising English cooks developed many other variations of fillings for these 'cheesecakes', such as ground almonds, breadcrumbs, ground rice, or, as in this case, mashed potatoes.

For the pastry:
175g/6oz plain flour
40g/1½ oz butter or margarine
40g/1½ oz lard
A pinch of salt
About 3 dessertspoonfuls
 of cold water

For the filling:
225g/8oz hot cooked potatoes
A pinch of salt
A pinch of nutmeg
115g/4oz softened butter
 or margarine
115g/4oz caster sugar
2 eggs, well-beaten
Grated rind & juice of 1 lemon

First put the potatoes on to cook – steamed or pressure-cooked potatoes are best, but otherwise boil them until they are tender. Whilst the potatoes are cooking, make the pastry. Rub the fats into the flour and salt until the mixture resembles fine breadcrumbs. Mix in just enough water to form a firm dough. Knead the dough lightly until it is smooth and pliable, then roll it out on a floured surface and use it to line an 20-22cm (8-9 inch) diameter flan tin. Prick all over the pastry on the base of the tin with a fork. Leave to rest in the fridge whilst you mix the filling.

Pre-heat the oven to 200°C/400°F/Gas Mark 6 and place a baking tray in the oven to heat up.

Mash the drained, hot potatoes with the salt and nutmeg, then pass them through a sieve to make a smooth purée. Add the butter or margarine, sugar, eggs, grated lemon rind and lemon juice. Beat thoroughly together. Fill the pastry-lined flan tin almost to the top with the mixture. Place the flan tin on the hot baking tray (this helps the pastry base to cook through) and bake on the middle shelf of the pre-heated oven for 15 minutes, then remove the potato cake from the flan tin, place on the baking tray and bake for a further 10-15 minutes until the pastry is crisp and the filling is set and browning on top.

The Old Hall at Gainsborough is a 15th-century manor house containing the most complete medieval kitchen in the country. In the 16th century it was the home of Henry VIII's sixth wife, Katherine Parr, when she was married to her first husband, Edward de Burgh, second Baron Borough of Gainsborough.

GAINSBOROUGH, THE OLD HALL c1955 G145001

RECIPE

LINCOLNSHIRE CARROT PUDDING

This is another old Lincolnshire recipe using a root vegetable to make a sweet dessert dish, in this case using carrots in a fruity steamed pudding that makes a good light alternative to a traditional Christmas Pudding.

> 115g/4oz plain flour
> 115g/4oz shredded suet
> 115g/4oz raisins
> 115g/4oz currants
> 115g/4oz grated raw potato
> 115g/4oz grated raw carrot
> 115g/4oz demerara sugar
> 115g/4oz fresh breadcrumbs
> ½ teaspoonful bicarbonate of soda
> 1 teaspoonful ground mixed spice
> 25g/1oz chopped glace cherries
> 1 large egg (beaten)
> A little milk for mixing, if necessary

In a large bowl, mix together the flour, bicarbonate of soda and mixed spice. Add all the other dry ingredients and mix it all well together. Add the beaten egg and mix it in to bind the mixture, adding a little milk if necessary. Put the mixture into a large, greased pudding basin, making sure that space is left at the top as the mixture will expand during cooking. Cover the basin with a double layer of pleated greaseproof paper and a piece of foil, and tie down firmly with string. Place the pudding basin in a large saucepan of boiling water and cover with the saucepan lid. Steam for 3 hours, topping up the saucepan with more boiling water from time to time to ensure that the pan does not boil dry. When cooked, turn out the pudding onto a warm serving dish and serve piping hot, with custard, cream or brandy sauce.

RECIPE

APPLE FLORENTINE PIE

This dish was traditionally made at Christmas-time in Lincolnshire in the past.

225g/8oz plain flour
115g/4oz butter or margarine
¼ teaspoonful salt
50ml/2 fl oz very cold water
4 large cooking apples
3 tablespoonfuls demerara sugar
1 tablespoonful grated lemon peel

50g/2oz sultanas
600ml/1 pint pale ale
¼ teaspoonful grated nutmeg
¼ teaspoonful cinnamon
3 cloves
Whipped cream, to serve

Pre-heat the oven to 200°C/400°F/Gas Mark 6. Make the pastry by mixing the salt and flour lightly together and rubbing in the butter or margarine until the mixture resembles fine breadcrumbs. Mix with enough cold water to form a soft dough. Roll out to 1cm (½ inch thick) on a floured board. Peel and core the apples, stand them in a deep, buttered ovenproof pie dish and sprinkle with 2 tablespoonfuls of the sugar and 1 teaspoonful of the grated lemon peel. Fill the centre of each apple with sultanas. Cover the dish with the pastry and bake in the pre-heated oven for 30 minutes. Heat together, but do not boil, the ale, nutmeg, cinnamon, cloves and remaining sugar. Remove the pie dish from the oven, carefully loosen the pastry crust and lift the pastry off the apples. Pour the ale mixture over the apples. Put each apple into a bowl, cut the pastry into 4 pieces and place one piece on top of each apple. Serve very hot, with whipped cream.

It was the custom in Lincolnshire in the past for poor people to go around begging for Christmas fare on St Thomas's Day – 21st December. This became known as 'Mumping Day' – 'mumping' is an old word meaning to beg or scrounge.

LOUTH, THE VIEW FROM THE WOLDS c1955 L305014

Harvest time is the most important time of the farming calendar, when the crops are gathered in and stored for use during the winter. In the past, the extra farmworkers who came to work on the farms at harvest time had to be fed, and the cake on the opposite page helped satisfy their hunger during the mid-day and afternoon breaks. In past times the thrifty housewife never wasted anything, and this recipe uses dripping, the rendered fat that drips from a joint of meat such as beef, lamb or mutton during roasting and can then be cooled and saved for other uses, such as pastry making. Clarified dripping will not make the cake taste of meat, but if you don't want to use this traditional ingredient, or if dripping is hard to obtain, modern cooks can use either lard, a hard vegetable baking fat like Cookeen, or butter or margarine as an alternative.

RECIPE

LINCOLNSHIRE FARMHOUSE DRIPPING CAKE

225g/8oz plain flour (this works well with wholemeal
as well as white flour)
Half a level teaspoonful of salt
50g/2oz chopped candied peel
225g/8oz raisins
175g/6oz sugar
115g/4oz clarified dripping (or alternative fat –
see opposite page)
1 tablespoonful of black treacle
150ml/5fl oz/ ¼ pint milk
2 eggs, beaten
1 tablespoonful extra milk
1 level teaspoonful bicarbonate of soda

Pre-heat the oven to 180°C/350°F/Gas Mark 4. Grease an 18-20cm (8-9 inch) round or square cake tin, and line it with greaseproof paper.
Put the sugar, dripping (or alternative fat) and black treacle into
a saucepan with the milk, and heat gently until it is all dissolved.
Remove from the heat and leave to cool for a few minutes.
Sift the flour into a mixing bowl with the salt. Add the chopped
candied peel and raisins. Stir the beaten eggs into the flour mixture
and mix well, then gradually mix in the milk and treacle mixture, a
little at a time and beating well after each addition, to make a soft,
dropping consistency. Dissolve the bicarbonate of soda in the extra
tablespoonful of milk, add to the mixture and stir it all together well.
Turn the mixture into the prepared cake tin. Bake in the pre-heated
oven for 1 hour, then reduce the oven temperature to 160°C/325°F/
Gas Mark 3 and cook for a further 20-30 minutes, until the cake is
risen and firm and a skewer inserted into the centre comes out clean.
Leave in the tin to settle for 5 minutes, then turn out onto a wire tray
to cool completely.

RECIPE

LINCOLNSHIRE PLUM BREAD

'Plum' in recipes usually means dried fruit such as currants, raisins and sultanas, but in this recipe plums are indeed used, albeit in their dried form as prunes. This is especially good if the dried fruit is soaked overnight in cold (milkless) tea before cooking.

> 450g/1 lb plain flour (strong breadmaking flour is best)
> 225g/8oz prunes, cut into small pieces
> 115ml/4fl oz milk, warm
> 115g/4oz butter, melted
> 4 tablespoonfuls caster sugar
> 50g/2oz currants
> 50g/2oz sultanas
> 15g/ ½ oz dried yeast
> 2 eggs, lightly beaten
> 1 teaspoonful ground cinnamon
> 1 teaspoonful ground allspice
> 1 pinch of salt

Mix together the milk, sugar, butter, yeast, beaten egg, salt, and spices. Add the flour, and beat the mixture until it is smooth, to make a soft pliable dough. Turn out the dough onto a floured surface, and knead until it is smooth and elastic. Place the dough in a bowl, cover, and leave to stand in a warm place until the dough has doubled in size. Knock back the dough and knead it again briefly, adding the dried fruit and making sure that it is evenly distributed. Divide the dough into two pieces, and place into two 450g (1 lb) greased and lined loaf tins. Cover and leave again in a warm place to rise until doubled in size. Pre-heat the oven to 190°C/375°F/Gas Mark 5. Place the loaf tins on a pre-heated baking sheet and bake for 40-50 minutes, then remove the loaves from the tins and return them to the oven to cook for a further 5-10 minutes, or until they sound hollow when tapped on the base. Store the loaves in an airtight container and serve in slices, spread with butter. This also makes excellent toast.

ALFORD, THE FIVE SAIL MILL c1955   A209313

Lincolnshire once had over 700 windmills. This shows one of the county's surviving mills, at Alford, at the foot of the Lincolnshire Wolds about 13 miles (21 km) north-west of Skegness. This is a beautifully proportioned six-storey, five-sail Lincolnshire ogee-capped windmill, located on the A1104 road. Built in 1837 by Sam Oxley, an Alford millwright, it is still in working order and regularly opened to the public.

RECIPE

GRANTHAM GINGERBREAD BALLS

In the south-west of Lincolnshire, the town of Grantham is famous for a special type of gingerbread. The recipe is said to have been devised by mistake when a local baker in the 1740s was making Grantham Whetstones, a type of flat hard biscuits, and added the wrong ingredients to the mixture. Unlike other gingerbreads, the Grantham version does not contain black treacle and so is known as a 'white' gingerbread. Traditionally the ginger flavour is strong, so use as much ginger as you prefer.

> 450g/1 lb plain flour
> 450g/1 lb caster sugar
> 225g/8oz butter
> 1 egg, beaten
> 1 teaspoonful baking powder
> Half a teaspoonful bicarbonate of soda
> 1-2 level teaspoonfuls ground ginger, to taste

Pre-heat the oven to 160°C/300°F/Gas Mark 2.

In a large bowl, cream the butter, gradually adding the sugar, and beat until light and fluffy. Stir the beaten egg into the mixture. Gradually fold in the sieved flour, bicarbonate of soda, baking powder and ground ginger to the mixture.

Form the mixture into small balls and flatten each on to ungreased baking sheets. Bake in the pre-heated over for 20 minutes or until they are light brown – do not let them cook until they are very dark. This recipe makes about 50-60 gingerbread balls.

46

This 1950s' photograph of Grantham shows the Bee Hive Inn on the left. Perched in the tree outside the inn is what is still one of the most famous sights in Grantham, the 'living sign' of a real bee hive, complete with a resident colony of honey bees. The pub is one of the oldest in the town, and there has been a bee hive in a tree there since the early 1700s. The poem on the wooden sign pointing to it reads:

> *Stop Traveller this wondrous sign explore,*
> *And say when thou hast viewed it o'er and o'er,*
> *Grantham now two rarities are thine,*
> *A lofty Steeple and a living sign.*

The 'lofty Steeple' is of St Wulfram's Church, in the background of this view. A glorious example of English Gothic style, its west front, including the tower and spire, was started around 1280. This was the first spire of the period to reach such a great height – nearly 283 feet high.

GRANTHAM, THE BEE HIVE INN c1955 G43051

GRANTHAM, ST PETER'S HILL
1904 51632

At the south end of Grantham's High Street the road widens to a pleasant green, formerly a market place. At its south end is an 1891 statue of Frederick Tollemache, the town's MP for nearly 50 years in the 19th century, from 1826. In the 20th century, Grantham was the birthplace in 1925 of Margaret Thatcher, Britain's first woman Prime Minister. Her father ran a grocer's shop in North Parade in the town.

RECIPE

FEN COUNTRY APPLE CAKE

225g/8oz shortcrust or puff pastry
750g/1½ lbs cooking apples
Juice of half a lemon
25g/1oz butter or margarine
50g/2oz caster sugar
2 rounded tablespoonfuls of semolina
25g/1oz currants
3 tablespoonfuls of black treacle

Peel, core and slice the apples. Put the apples, lemon juice and butter into a pan, cover, and simmer slowly until pulpy. Add the sugar and semolina, and bring slowly to the boil. Cook gently for five minutes or until the mixture has thickened. Remove from the heat and leave until completely cold.

Pre-heat the oven to 220°C/425°F/Gas Mark 7 and grease an 18-20cm (7-8 inch) heatproof pie plate or dish.

Divide the pastry into two pieces. Roll out one portion and use it to line the prepared pie plate or dish. Spread with half the apple filling to within half an inch of the edges. Sprinkle with currants and add the treacle, and then top with the remaining filling.

Roll out the rest of the pastry into a 22-24cm (8-9 inch) round, moisten the edges with water and cover the pie. Press the edges well together to seal them, and knock up with the back of a knife. Brush the top with beaten egg or milk and then bake towards the top of the pre-heated oven for 25-30 minutes or until pale gold in colour.

RECIPE

LINCOLN GINGER BISCUITS

350g/12oz self-raising flour
225g/8oz sugar
2 teaspoonfuls bicarbonate of soda
115g/4oz butter or margarine
2 teaspoonfuls ground ginger
2 teaspoonfuls golden syrup
1 beaten egg

Pre-heat the oven to180°C/350°F/Gas Mark 4

Place all the dry ingredients in a bowl.

Heat the butter or margarine and golden syrup gently in a pan until the fat has melted, then pour over the dry ingredients and mix it all to a fairly stiff consistency, whilst slowly adding in the beaten egg.

Roll small pieces of the dough in your hand to make balls about the size of a walnut.

Place each ball of dough on a greased baking sheet, making sure they are well spaced apart. Bake in the pre-heated oven for 15-20 minutes until the biscuits are golden brown.

FRANCIS FRITH

PIONEER VICTORIAN PHOTOGRAPHER

Francis Frith, founder of the world-famous photographic archive, was a complex and multi-talented man. A devout Quaker and a highly successful Victorian businessman, he was philosophical by nature and pioneering in outlook. By 1855 he had already established a wholesale grocery business in Liverpool, and sold it for the astonishing sum of £200,000, which is the equivalent today of over £15,000,000. Now in his thirties, and captivated by the new science of photography, Frith set out on a series of pioneering journeys up the Nile and to the Near East.

INTRIGUE AND EXPLORATION

He was the first photographer to venture beyond the sixth cataract of the Nile. Africa was still the mysterious 'Dark Continent', and Stanley and Livingstone's historic meeting was a decade into the future. The conditions for picture taking confound belief. He laboured for hours in his wicker dark-room in the sweltering heat of the desert, while the volatile chemicals fizzed dangerously in their trays. Back in London he exhibited his photographs and was 'rapturously cheered' by members of the Royal Society. His reputation as a photographer was made overnight.

VENTURE OF A LIFE-TIME

By the 1870s the railways had threaded their way across the country, and Bank Holidays and half-day Saturdays had been made obligatory by Act of Parliament. All of a sudden the working man and his family were able to enjoy days out, take holidays, and see a little more of the world.

With typical business acumen, Francis Frith foresaw that these new tourists would enjoy having souvenirs to commemorate their days out. For the next thirty years he travelled the country by train and by pony and trap, producing fine photographs of seaside resorts and beauty spots that were keenly bought by millions of Victorians. These prints were painstakingly pasted into family albums and pored over during the dark nights of winter, rekindling precious memories of summer excursions. Frith's studio was soon supplying retail shops all over the country, and by 1890 F Frith & Co had become the greatest specialist photographic publishing company in the world, with over 2,000 sales outlets, and pioneered the picture postcard.

FRANCIS FRITH'S LEGACY

Francis Frith had died in 1898 at his villa in Cannes, his great project still growing. By 1970 the archive he created contained over a third of a million pictures showing 7,000 British towns and villages.

Frith's legacy to us today is of immense significance and value, for the magnificent archive of evocative photographs he created provides a unique record of change in the cities, towns and villages throughout Britain over a century and more. Frith and his fellow studio photographers revisited locations many times down the years to update their views, compiling for us an enthralling and colourful pageant of British life and character.

We are fortunate that Frith was dedicated to recording the minutiae of everyday life. For it is this sheer wealth of visual data, the painstaking chronicle of changes in dress, transport, street layouts, buildings, housing and landscape that captivates us so much today, offering us a powerful link with the past and with the lives of our ancestors.

Computers have now made it possible for Frith's many thousands of images to be accessed almost instantly. The archive offers every one of us an opportunity to examine the places where we and our families have lived and worked down the years. Its images, depicting our shared past, are now bringing pleasure and enlightenment to millions around the world a century and more after his death.

For further information visit: www.francisfrith.com

INTERIOR DECORATION

Frith's photographs can be seen framed and as giant wall murals in thousands of pubs, restaurants, hotels, banks, retail stores and other public buildings throughout Britain. These provide interesting and attractive décor, generating strong local interest and acting as a powerful reminder of gentler days in our increasingly busy and frenetic world.

FRITH PRODUCTS

All Frith photographs are available as prints and posters in a variety of different sizes and styles. In the UK we also offer a range of other gift and stationery products illustrated with Frith photographs, although many of these are not available for delivery outside the UK – see our web site for more information on the products available for delivery in your country.

THE INTERNET

Over 100,000 photographs of Britain can be viewed and purchased on the Frith web site. The web site also includes memories and reminiscences contributed by our customers, who have personal knowledge of localities and of the people and properties depicted in Frith photographs. If you wish to learn more about a specific town or village you may find these reminiscences fascinating to browse. Why not add your own comments if you think they would be of interest to others? See **www.francisfrith.com**

PLEASE HELP US BRING FRITH'S PHOTOGRAPHS TO LIFE

Our authors do their best to recount the history of the places they write about. They give insights into how particular towns and villages developed, they describe the architecture of streets and buildings, and they discuss the lives of famous people who lived there. But however knowledgeable our authors are, the story they tell is necessarily incomplete.

Frith's photographs are so much more than plain historical documents. They are living proofs of the flow of human life down the generations. They show real people at real moments in history; and each of those people is the son or daughter of someone, the brother or sister, aunt or uncle, grandfather or grandmother of someone else. All of them lived, worked and played in the streets depicted in Frith's photographs.

We would be grateful if you would give us your insights into the places shown in our photographs: the streets and buildings, the shops, businesses and industries. Post your memories of life in those streets on the Frith website: what it was like growing up there, who ran the local shop and what shopping was like years ago; if your workplace is shown tell us about your working day and what the building is used for now. Read other visitors' memories and reconnect with your shared local history and heritage. With your help more and more Frith photographs can be brought to life, and vital memories preserved for posterity, and for the benefit of historians in the future.

Wherever possible, we will try to include some of your comments in future editions of our books. Moreover, if you spot errors in dates, titles or other facts, please let us know, because our archive records are not always completely accurate—they rely on 140 years of human endeavour and hand-compiled records. You can email us using the contact form on the website.

Thank you!

For further information, trade, or author enquiries
please contact us at the address below:

**The Francis Frith Collection, Oakley Business Park,
Wylye Road, Dinton, Wiltshire SP3 5EU England.**
Tel: +44 (0)1722 716 376 Fax: +44 (0)1722 716 881
e-mail: sales@francisfrith.co.uk **www.francisfrith.com**